Numbers

Contents

 **Look and put the sticker.**

one

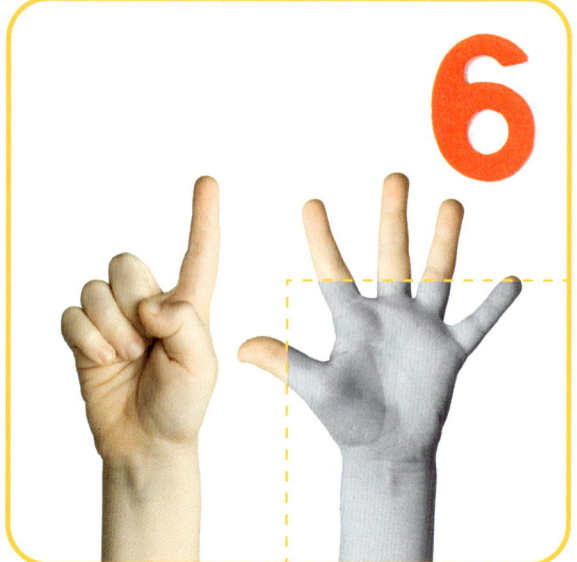

six

four

three

 Put sticker on the word.

How old are you?

I'm [four].

 Ask and say.

 Color and say.

three

one

four

six

three

five

one

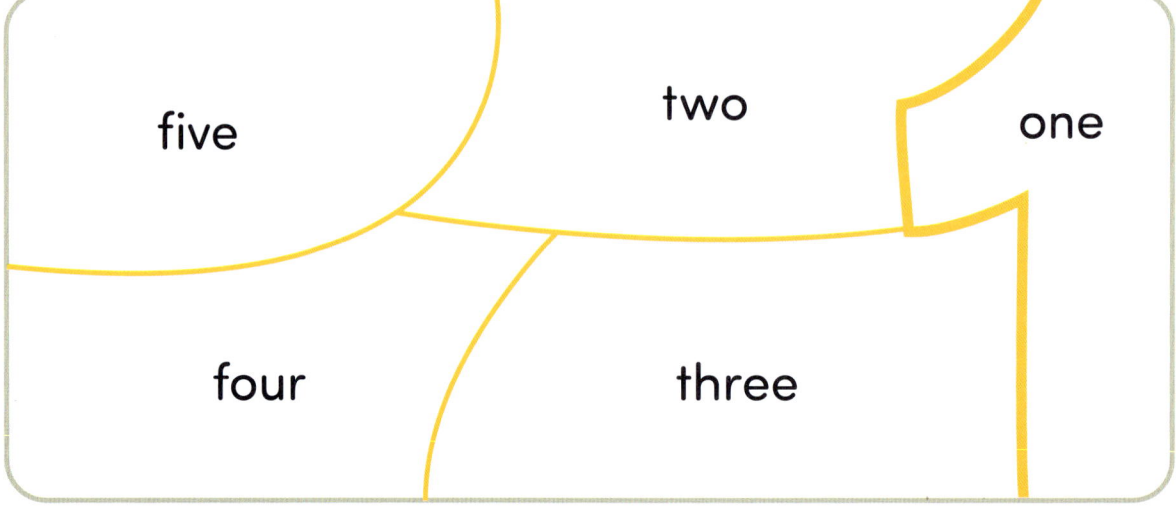

five

two

one

four

three

 **Look and put the sticker.**

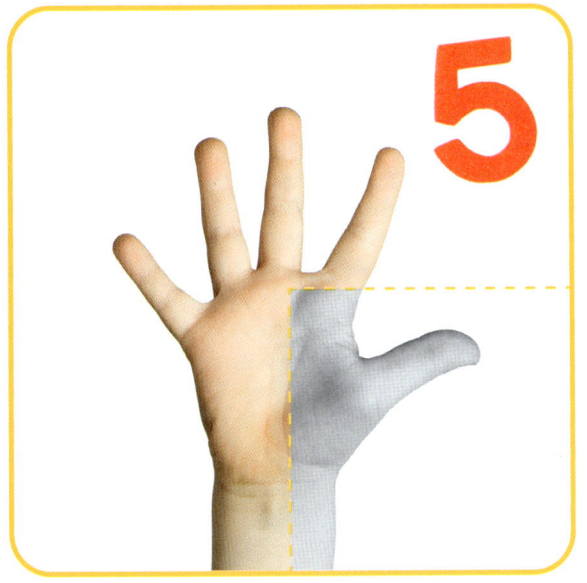

five

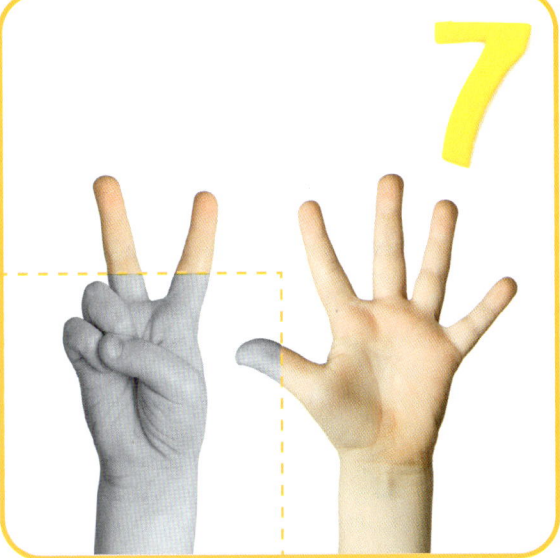

seven

eight

two

 **Put sticker on the word.**

How old are you?

5

I'm [five] .

 Ask and say.

 p. 2

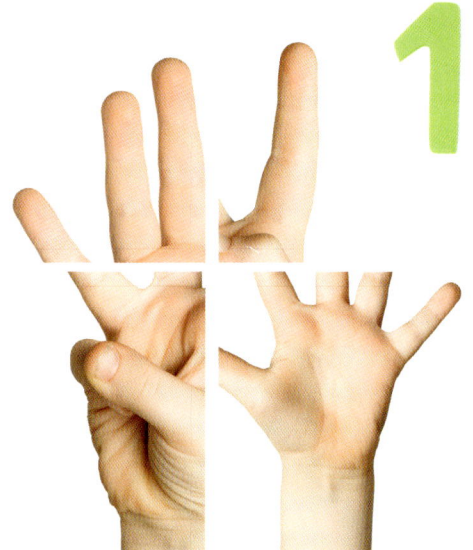

1

 p. 3

four

 p. 5

2

 p. 6

five

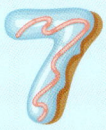  

Let's Draw

 Draw the number.

two

six

Let's Have Fun

Sticker

Put the cookies in the jar.

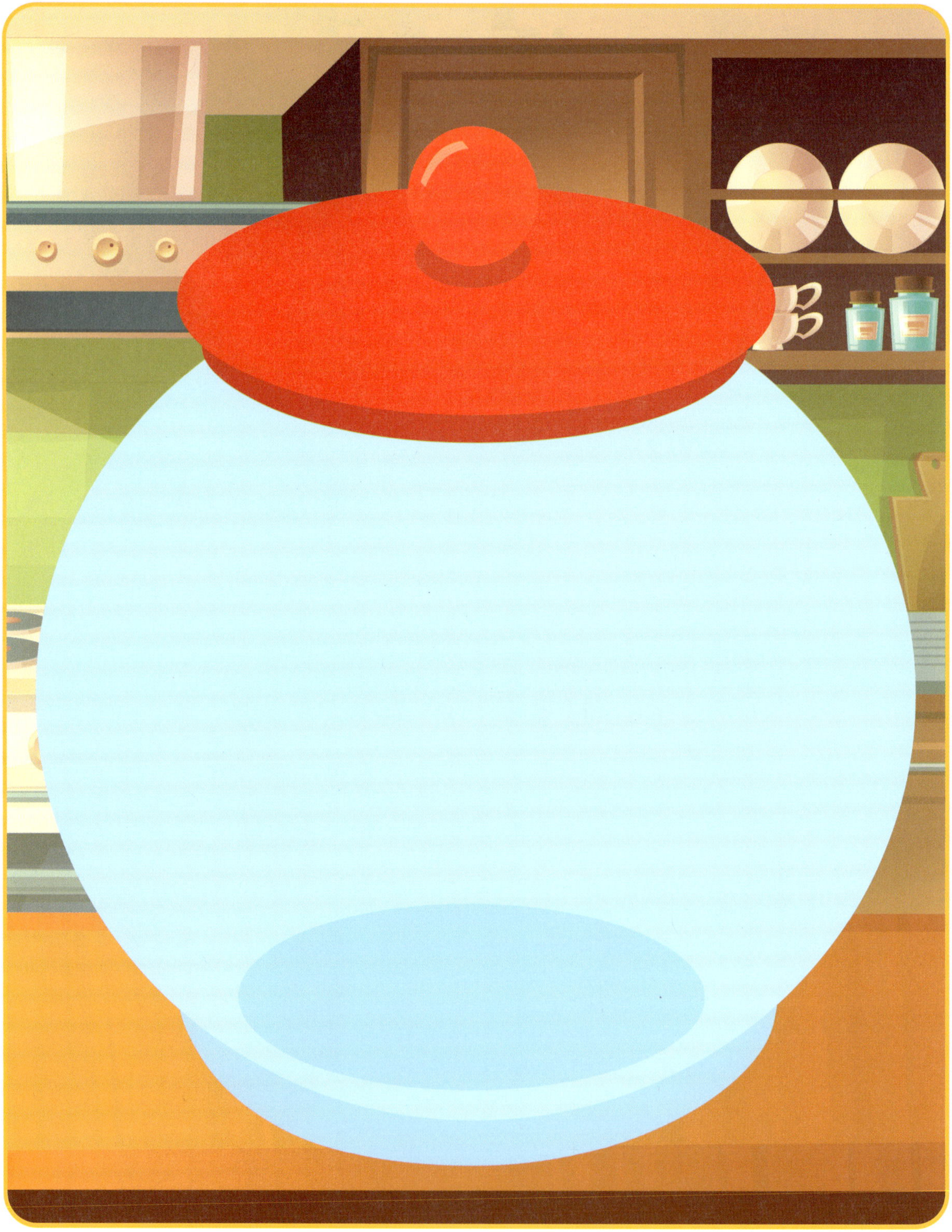

1

2

3

4

two

one

four

three

5

6

7

8

six

five

eight

seven